Understanding the Elements of the Periodic Table™

CALCIUM

Greg Roza

20

40

Ca

rosen publishing's
**rosen
central**®

New York

Published in 2008 by The Rosen Publishing Group, Inc.
29 East 21st Street, New York, NY 10010

First Edition

Library of Congress Cataloging-in-Publication Data

Roza, Greg.
Calcium / Greg Roza.
    p. cm.—(Understanding the elements of the periodic table)
Includes bibliographical references and index.
ISBN-13: 978-1-4042-1963-2
ISBN-10: 1-4042-1963-3
1. Calcium—Juvenile literature. 2. Periodic law—Tables—Juvenile literature.
3. Chemical elements—Juvenile literature. I. Title.
QD181.C2R69 2008
546'.393—dc22

2007000033

Manufactured in China

On the cover: Calcium's square on the periodic table of elements. Inset: The atomic structure of calcium.

Contents

Introduction

Have you ever heard the phrase "in the limelight"? Have you ever wondered what a limelight is? "Lime" has been used as a general name for a number of natural materials that contain the element calcium in its ionic form, but "lime" now technically refers only to calcium oxide (CaO). In the early 1800s, English inventor Goldsworthy Gurney discovered that calcium oxide glows with a brilliant light when placed in a flame fueled by burning hydrogen and oxygen gases. A Scottish engineer named Thomas Drummond saw a demonstration of this effect in 1825. He instantly realized useful applications for the intense light. He developed the first limelight to be used by surveyors. The light produced by early limelight could be seen from more than 60 miles (96.5 kilometers) away!

Although Drummond's invention was initially used by surveyors, other uses quickly became evident. Limelight was used in nineteenth-century lighthouses. In 1837, the Covent Garden Theatre in London, England, installed limelight to illuminate the stage. Actors were literally standing "in the limelight," or in the bright glow shed by limelight. After that, it became popular lighting in theaters around the world. It was particularly popular in the 1860s and 1870s. The advent of electricity and electrical lighting took the place of limelight. Still, it had made a lasting impact on modern culture. Today, the phrase "in the limelight" is still used to describe people who are in the public eye or at the center of attention.

Limelight is just one of many purposes that calcium compounds have been used for over the centuries. Calcium materials such as concrete and mortars have been essential components in the construction of buildings and roads since the ancient Egyptians used gypsum ($CaSO_4 \bullet 2H_2O$) to make mortars to build the pyramids. Calcium ion is also vital to human growth and wellness.

Chapter One
What Is Calcium?

Calcium is the fifth most abundant element in Earth's crust and is always found in ionic form in compounds. Calcium compounds exist in many environments all over the world. Human beings have known about calcium compounds for centuries. Ancient Romans used an abundant calcium source called limestone. Limestone contains the most common calcium compound, calcium carbonate ($CaCO_3$). Calcium carbonate comes most often in the form of calcite, a crystal. This is the most stable form of calcium carbonate. Calcite is found in the ground worldwide and makes up the shells of many marine organisms.

The History of Calcium

The Romans discovered that by heating limestone, they could create calcium oxide (CaO), a white, chalky substance. Calcium oxide is caustic (basic). The Greeks called this substance calx. This is where the word "calcium" came from. Today, we also refer to calcium oxide (or calcium oxide/magnesium oxide mixtures) as lime or quick lime.

The ancient Romans and Greeks used lime to create mortar. Mortar—a soft mixture that hardens as it dries—is still used to hold stones and bricks together. The Romans mixed lime with water and sand to make mortar. This mixture was used to build many structures.

This third-century CE Roman wall once surrounded the city of Verulamium. The Romans built many structures like this one out of calcium-based mortar.

By adding water to lime, the Romans created calcium hydroxide ($Ca(OH)_2$). The common names for calcium hydroxide are slaked lime or hydrated lime. Calcium hydroxide is an alkaline or base. It is used as a fertilizer, a sewage treatment chemical, and an ingredient in mortars and plasters.

The ancient Romans knew that when limestone was heated, it changed into a new substance. They also knew that this new substance, lime, weighed less than the limestone that they started with, but they did not know why. In 1754, a British chemist named Joseph Black discovered that limestone loses weight because the compound loses an invisible gas as it

Davy's Method

Calcium was first isolated by English chemist Sir Humphry Davy. He first isolated potassium metal, followed by sodium metal, in 1807. In 1808, he isolated calcium, barium, strontium, and magnesium metals. But how was he able to do this? The answer is through electrolysis.

Electrolysis is the process of passing an electrical current (i.e., electrons) through compounds. This process causes chemical reactions that involve the addition and subtraction of electrons in components of the compounds. For example, a metal ion (which is positively charged) may gain one or more electrons to form the neutral elemental or metal form of the element. At first, electrolysis was used to look for reactions to form elements using substances that were previously believed to be elemental.

Davy prepared a mixture of lime and mercury (II) oxide (HgO). By electrolyzing the mixture, he produced a small amount of impure calcium. However, there was not enough calcium to experiment with the first time around. So Davy tried the experiment again and created enough nearly pure calcium to conduct some basic tests to learn more about the newly discovered element.

His and others' work with electrolysis led to the branch of science called electrochemistry. This is the science that studies the reactions between electricity and chemical substances. Davy was rewarded for his discoveries. In 1812, he was knighted by King George III of England. The following year, he traveled to France and received a medal from French leader Napoleon Bonaparte.

This portrait of Sir Humphry Davy was completed around 1805, a few years before he successfully isolated nearly pure calcium metal.

is heated. This invisible gas is carbon dioxide (CO_2), although Black did not know the identity of it at the time. Black also showed that the gas reentered the lime when the lime was exposed to air for extended periods of time. Eventually, this turns the calcium oxide back into calcium carbonate, or limestone.

The Periodic Table

The periodic table is a convenient organizational chart of all the known elements. In 1869, Russian chemist Dmitry Mendeleyev came up with a form of the periodic table that is similar to the one we are familiar with today. Other scientists had already developed their own ways of organizing and displaying the known elements. However, Mendeleyev's table was the most useful; it grouped elements based on similar characteristics, particularly atomic weight. Once this was done, Mendeleyev and other scientists noticed that elements with like characteristics could be arranged in regular intervals, or periods. They left blanks in their periodic tables where they predicted other elements would appear once they were discovered. The periodic table has changed over the years, but it is still based on Mendeleyev's original concept.

As of 2007, the periodic table features 117 elements. Occasionally scientists discover new ones; all new elements are now made in the laboratory and most are stable for only part of a second! The newest chemical element is number 118, currently referred to as ununoctium (you-nuh-NAHK-tee-uhm). The synthesis of a new element needs to be repeated more than once (which can take months or even years), preferably by more than one research group. The work is carefully scrutinized by other scientists before the report of the new element is approved for dissemination. For the element with atomic number 118, this process culminated in October 2006. The periodic table still contains a blank space where element 117 would reside, which scientists hope to fill one day. In addition, the synthesis of other elements with atomic numbers greater than 118 is a goal of scientists.

Calcium: A Unique Element

Calcium's place on the periodic table groups it with other elements that have similar properties. However, all chemical elements have unique traits that set them apart from each other. Calcium metal creates a brick-red flame when burned. Pure calcium metal is usually a relatively soft, silver-gray solid. Pure calcium metal reacts quickly with air, water, and other elements that can accept electrons such as the halogens (fluorine on down) to form numerous compounds. For this reason, calcium metal is never found pure in nature. The calcium ion is also the mineral that our bodies need in the greatest quantity to stay healthy.

An ion is an atom with a positive or negative electrical charge. Atoms of elemental calcium easily lose two electrons. This turns them into positive ions with a +2 charge. Calcium ions are attracted to negatively charged ions found in solutions. If the resulting compound has limited solubility, then a solid calcium compound is formed that sinks to

This small pile of pure calcium is silvery-gray. When exposed to air, a white coating called nitride quickly forms on the surface of pure calcium.

the bottom of the solution. This new solid compound is called a precipitate. Because of this unique trait (limited solubility of its compounds), calcium ion sometimes is used to remove impurities (negative ions) from solutions.

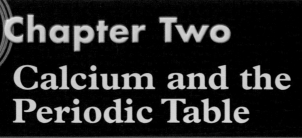

Chapter Two
Calcium and the Periodic Table

An element is something that cannot be broken down into other substances by ordinary chemical or physical means. Pure chemical elements, such as calcium metal, are made up of very tiny building blocks called atoms. Atoms are incredibly small—so small, in fact, that it would take about 25,000,000 calcium atoms to make a line about 1 centimeter long. Atoms are so small they cannot be seen, even with a microscope. Despite this, scientists have determined that atoms are made up of even smaller pieces called subatomic particles.

Subatomic Particles

There are three types of subatomic particles that determine the chemical properties of an atom (physicists have shown that there are additional particles, for instance, making up the nucleons): protons, neutrons, and electrons. Protons have a positive electrical charge (+1 charge each). Neutrons do not have an electrical charge. Protons and neutrons group together to make up the nucleus—or core—of an atom. The nucleus makes up most of an atom's mass. The nucleus of an atom also has a positive electrical charge because of the protons. Since most of the atom's mass is found in the nucleus, and the nucleus occupies only a tiny fraction of the atom, the nucleus is extremely dense.

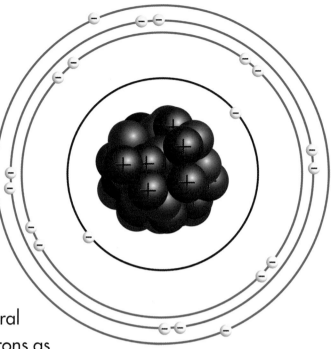

This is an illustration of the structure of calcium. It shows the protons and neutrons in the nucleus, and the electrons orbiting in shells, or layers, around the nucleus.

Electrons are negatively charged particles (–1 charge each). They reside around the nucleus in overlapping layers called shells. Each layer contains a specific number of electrons; that number depends on the specific shell. Electrons have very little mass. Neutral atoms have the same number of electrons as they do protons. This gives these atoms no overall electrical charge. An atom that gains one or more extra electrons has a negative charge equal to the number of electrons the neutral atoms gains. An atom that loses one or more electrons has a positive charge; the charge is equal to the number of electrons lost from the neutral atom. These electrically charged atoms are ions. Positive ions are cations, and negative ions are anions. Ions are capable of conducting electricity. This makes them important to the proper functioning of the human body. The muscles, for example, need calcium ions and other ions to contract and relax.

The identity of a chemical element is determined by the number of protons that it contains. Elements that differ in only a single proton or two, a change that seems very small, are vastly different from each other in properties. For example, most calcium atoms have twenty protons, twenty neutrons, and twenty electrons. At room temperature, pure calcium is a relatively soft, silvery metal. Argon—chemical element number 18—usually has eighteen protons, twenty-two neutrons, and eighteen electrons. Despite these minute differences, argon is a colorless gas at room temperature.

Categorizing Chemical Elements

The modern periodic table is a convenient way of categorizing the chemical elements. Starting with hydrogen, the elements are listed in order of their atomic numbers. This is the number of protons found in the nucleus of an atom. The atomic number for calcium is twenty because its nucleus contains twenty protons.

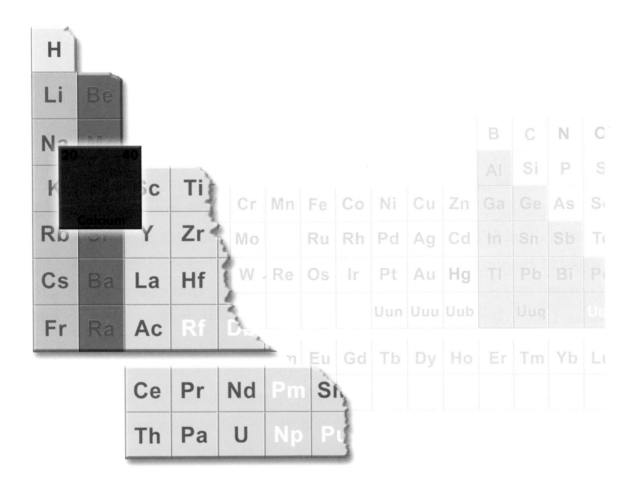

"Ca" is the scientific symbol for calcium. The 20 in the upper left corner is calcium's atomic number. The number 40 in the upper right corner is calcium's atomic weight.

Chemical elements have been categorized by their atomic weights (for instance, in early periodic tables, like the one promoted by Mendeleyev). Another name for atomic weight is atomic mass. This is a measure of the mass of a single atom. The atomic weight of calcium is usually given as 40, although it is listed on periodic tables as 40.078. This is because of calcium's isotopes. Isotopes are versions of an element with a different number of neutrons. Calcium has twenty-four known isotopes; some occur naturally, and others are only made in the laboratory. When the atomic weights of the six naturally occurring isotopes are averaged together and weighted for their natural abundances, the result is 40.078. About 97 percent of the calcium that occurs in nature is in an isotope called calcium 40 (Ca-40). Along with argon 40 (Ar-40), Ca-40 is an end product of the decay of potassium 40 (K-40), a radioactive isotope.

Groups and Periods

The modern periodic table organizes the elements by increasing atomic number and by grouping elements with similar properties together.

The columns of the periodic table are known as groups. The first column on the left side of the table is Group 1. This group is also called the alkali metals, all of which are soft, silvery metals that react easily with other elements that can accept one or more electrons to form compounds with a +1 charged alkali metal ion. The next group is Group 2, or the alkaline earth metals. Calcium belongs to this group. All alkaline earth metals are relatively soft, silvery-gray metals that react easily with other elements and compounds that can accept electrons to form compounds with a +2 charged alkaline earth metal ion.

Elements can be described by the row in which they appear. These rows are called periods. The number of each period tells us how many electron shells, or layers containing electrons, that each atom has. Calcium,

Group

1		1 H Hydrogen									

Period

	3 7 Li Lithium	4 9 Be Beryllium								Ni
2	11 23 Na Sodium	12 24 Mg Magnesium								
3	19 39 K Potassium	20 40 Ca Calcium	21 45 Sc Scandium	22 48 Ti Titanium	23 51 V Vanadium	24 52 Cr Chromium	25 55 Mn Manganese	26 56 Fe Iron	27 59 Co Cobalt	Ni
4	37 85 Rb Rubidium	38 88 Sr Strontium	39 89 Y Yttrium	40 91 Zr Zirconium	41 93 Nb Niobium	42 96 Mo Molybdenum	43 98 Tc Technetium	44 101 Ru Ruthenium	45 103 Rh Rhodium	Pd
5	55 133 Cs Cesium	56 137 Ba Barium	57 139 La Lanthanum	72 178 Hf Hafnium	73 181 Ta Tantalum	74 184 W Tungsten	75 186 Re Rhenium	76 190 Os Osmium	77 192 Ir Iridium	Pt
6	87 223 Fr Francium	88 226 Ra Radium	89 227 Ac Actinium	104 261 Rf Rutherfordium	105 262 Db Dubnium	106 266 Sg Seaborgium	107 264 Bh Bohrium	108 277 Hs Hassium	109 268 Mt Meitnerium	
7										

58 140 Ce Cerium	59 141 Pr Praseodymium	60 144 Nd Neodymium	61 145 Pm Promethium	62 150 Sm Samarium	63 152 Eu Europium	64 157 Gd Gadolinium	Tb
90 232 Th Thorium	91 231 Pa Protactinium	92 238 U Uranium	93 237 Np Neptunium	94 244 Pu Plutonium	95 243 Am Americium	96 247 Cm Curium	

This section of the periodic table shows that calcium is the third chemical element in Group 2. It also illustrates that calcium is the second chemical element in Period 4.

for example, is in Period 4. All elements in Period 4 have four electron shells. Elements farther to the right in a period have more electrons than those to the left, but they all have the same number of shells.

Calcium Ions

Calcium and other alkaline earth metals are more reactive than many other elements. This is because the two electrons that their atoms have in their outermost shells are easy to remove. When this happens, the resulting calcium ion is no longer reactive toward loss of electrons (no longer likely to react with another element). A calcium ion has two more protons than it has electrons. This gives it a positive charge of +2. The way scientists show the calcium ion in writing is Ca^{2+}. All calcium compounds contain this ion combined with enough anions (negatively charged ions) to form a neutral species.

Acids and Bases

Acids are compounds that contain hydrogen ions (H+) that are easily lost, for instance, in water. The more hydrogen ions an acid forms in water for the same amount of starting acid, the stronger the acid is. Bases—also called alkalis—are compounds that form hydroxide ions (OH−) in water. Hydroxide ions are made up of an atom of oxygen bound to an atom of hydrogen, plus an extra electron to give the group an overall negative charge. Depending on how strong and concentrated the solution is, acids and bases can be quite dangerous.

When combined in equal quantities, strong acid and alkaline compounds neutralize each other. This means that they form a compound that is neither acidic nor alkaline. Often, such acids and bases form water and a salt when combined.

Calcium Snapshot

20
Ca
40

Chemical Symbol:	Ca
Classification:	Alkaline earth metal
Properties:	Silvery-white and relatively soft; has the most isotopes of any element; most common metal ion in many animals, including human beings.
Isolated by:	Sir Humphry Davy
Atomic Number:	20
Atomic Weight:	40.078 atomic mass unit (amu)
Protons:	20
Electrons:	20
Neutrons:	20
Density at 68° Fahrenheit (20° Celsius):	1.55 g/cm^3
Melting Point:	1,542.2°F (839°C)
Boiling Point:	2,703.2°F (1,484°C)
Commonly Found:	In soil systems as limestone and gypsum.

The cloudy substance in this test tube is calcium hydroxide precipitate. This is a solid that forms when sodium hydroxide (NaOH) is added to a solution containing calcium ions.

Some calcium compounds are bases, although it depends on what anion is found with the calcium ion. Some basic compounds can be caustic. Calcium hydroxide [$Ca(OH)_2$], for example, is a common industrial chemical that is basic because it dissolves to form hydroxide ions in solution. Calcium hydroxide was once used to help break down dead organic material. Most calcium compounds are perfectly safe. Many foods, particularly dairy products, contain calcium ions.

Chapter Three
Calcium in the Natural World

Calcium is the fifth most abundant element in Earth's crust and the third most abundant metal after aluminum and iron. The most common calcium compound—calcium carbonate—exists in many natural minerals and materials, such as chalk, limestone, and marble. Calcium ions also can be found in many living creatures. Animal shells and bones—and human bones—are made up mostly of calcium ions. This is what makes them so hard and durable. Coral reefs, as well as the tiny animals that make them, have calcium ions in them. Pearls, which are made by clams and oysters, do, too.

Many millions of years ago, when Earth had just formed, calcium ions could be found in igneous rocks. Igneous rocks are those formed by volcanoes. Over time, these rocks broke down into clay and soil due to weathering. Rivers and streams carried calcium ions and other minerals into the oceans. As ancient seas evaporated and disappeared, thick layers of calcium carbonate and other minerals were left behind. The carbonate ions sometimes mixed with calcium and magnesium (Mg) ions during this process, creating what mineral geologists call calcium magnesium carbonate, or dolomite. The formula for dolomite is $CaMg(CO_3)_2$.

Many limestone deposits are the result of animal shells and bones building up over many years. Animals that live in the ocean use calcium ions from seawater to create shells and bones. When these animals die,

Coral is made by small sea creatures called polyps. Polyps produce calcium carbonate in liquid form. The liquid hardens around them, creating a beautiful shell of coral.

their shells and bones settle on the ocean floor. Over millions of years, these materials build up, leaving thick deposits of calcium carbonate. One form of limestone called chalk is made up of the skeletons of microscopic sea creatures. Chalk is softer and more crumbly than regular limestone. Shell fossils often can be found in deposits of limestone.

Calcium Carbonate

Calcium carbonate is by far the most abundant calcium compound on Earth. "Limestone" is the common word for rocks that contain calcium carbonate; these rocks frequently contain varying amounts of other alkaline earth metal ions such as Mg^{2+} as well. Limestone is a sedimentary rock. This means that it was made when solid substances settled to the bottom of a body of water. These deposits harden over millions of years due to heat and pressure caused by other layers of sediments on top of them.

Calcium compounds, particularly limestone, are commonly found in caves. These calcium compounds occur in layers over cave walls. The long, pointed columns that descend from cave ceilings (stalactites) or rise from cave floors (stalagmites) primarily are made up of the mineral calcite (a form of calcium carbonate or limestone). These limestone deposits build up over many years. As rainwater passes through soil, it picks up ions including calcium. Water containing calcium ions seeps into the caves and drips over the surfaces of the cave, which is often drier, causing part of the water to evaporate. Sometimes this calcium ion–containing water drips from the ceiling, one tiny drop at a time. After a while, the calcium

ions in this water precipitate (become solid) to build up the cave formations.

A similar process occurs around hot springs, such as Mammoth Hot Springs, Wyoming. As rainwater seeps into the ground, it dissolves minerals like calcium carbonate in the soil. Sometimes this water is heated in underground chambers. When this water reaches the

This is a view of a giant stone column at Carlsbad Caverns, New Mexico, made over millions of years as a stalactite and a stalagmite joined.

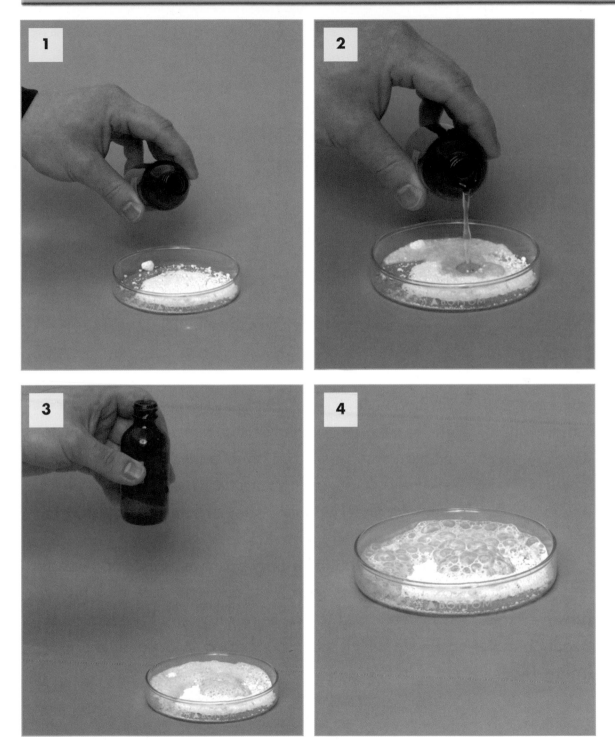

Place drops of lemon juice and/or vinegar on calcium carbonate (1 and 2). The calcium carbonate will bubble (3 and 4). This demonstrates how acid rain can quickly erode calcium rocks.

surface in hot-water springs and geysers, the water cools. This causes calcium carbonate to precipitate quickly as calcite crystals around the springs. Calcite can form beautiful, sparkling sheets and formations. Geysers can coat surrounding objects—such as rock and sticks—with a gleaming layer of calcite. This form of calcite is commonly called travertine.

Calcium Sulfate

Calcium sulfate ($CaSO_4$) is a mineral similar to calcium carbonate. Pure calcium sulfate is white in color, comes in several different forms, and is mined similar to the way calcium carbonate is mined. It is most often found in nature in the form of gypsum. Gypsum is a soft, chalky crystal that contains calcium sulfate along with two molecules of water ($CaSO_4 \bullet 2H_2O$). Often, it is called hydrous or hydrated calcium sulfate. "Hydrous" and "hydrated" both mean "containing water." Natural calcium sulfate without water can be found in a crystal mineral called anhydrite ($CaSO_4$). The name "anhydrite" is derived from "anhydrous," which means "without water." Anhydrite is found in nature as a white crystal. Gypsum and anhydrite are very common minerals. They are mined in many places around the world.

A less common, fine-grained form of gypsum is alabaster. Alabaster is a crystal that looks similar to marble. It can be white or white with brown streaks. It has been used in sculpture and carving because of its beauty and the ease with which it can be shaped. Most alabaster comes from various locations in England.

Metamorphic Rocks

Calcium compounds are abundant. Calcium compounds exist in vast deposits all over the world. Some deposits are near or on Earth's surface and can be reached easily. Others are deeper underground and require extensive blasting to be reached. Limestone sources are believed to be nearly inexhaustible. Marble is attained in block form from marble quarries.

The most commonly used calcium compound today is calcium carbonate. Most of the calcium carbonate used for industrial purposes is attained through mining. Not all mined sources of calcium carbonate are pure sources. Pure calcium carbonate is needed for the manufacture of food and medicinal products. To make pure calcium carbonate, carbon dioxide gas is added to a solution of calcium hydroxide. The carbon dioxide reacts with the calcium hydroxide to form calcium carbonate and water.

This is White Sands National Monument in New Mexico. The sand is actually gypsum. Gypsum sand is very rare because gypsum normally dissolves in water, but it thrives in this dry environment.

Despite the abundance of calcium compounds in the natural world, pure calcium metal is never found in nature. Calcium metal is too reactive and thus must be made in a laboratory under carefully controlled conditions that keep the calcium metal isolated from substances with which it will react. Today, pure calcium metal still is obtained through electrolysis. However, the process has changed since Davy pioneered it. It is electrolyzed from calcium chloride ($CaCl_2$) or calcium fluoride (CaF_2). Pure calcium metal is used for few purposes. It is sometimes used when refining other metals, such as uranium, or to remove oxygen, carbon, and sulfur from certain alloys.

Chapter Four
Calcium in Our World

Calcium compounds, particularly limestone, are among the most abundant industrial chemicals in use today. In addition to the purposes that we will discuss in this chapter, limestone and slaked lime (calcium hydroxide) are used in the manufacture of glass, fertilizer, soap, pesticides, and in sewage treatment. Other calcium compounds, such as gypsum, are widely used also. Most calcium compounds are inexpensive, plentiful, easy to cut into blocks, simple to shape, and last a long time.

Building with Calcium

Archaeologists in Turkey have discovered evidence that lime was used as a mortar approximately 7,000 years ago. Throughout the centuries, many cultures have used limestone and marble in building important and lasting structures. Up until the twentieth century, the most common use for lime was as an ingredient in concretes. Lime continues to be used in the construction industry, although it is utilized more often in industrial chemicals.

Marble

Marble has been used in building and sculpture since the time of the ancient Greeks. Marble is much harder and more expensive than limestone.

How Is Portland Cement Made?

Cement is a powdery substance that binds other substances together, making them stronger and perfect for building. One of the first effective cements was crushed limestone. Today, "cement" is the general term used for a gray powder made up mostly of calcium compounds, but also silicon, aluminum, and iron compounds.

The ancient Egyptians had a process of making cement that was forgotten during the Middle Ages. This process was discovered once again in 1824 by British bricklayer Joseph Aspdin. Limestone boulders are mined and placed in a large machine that crushes them into small rocks. Smaller amounts of clay and sand are mixed in with the limestone. These raw materials are ground into a fine powder. Next, the mixture is heated in a huge, rotating furnace to about 2,700°F (1,480°C). This is hot enough to cause chemical changes in the raw materials, but not hot enough to fully melt them. The mixture comes out of the furnace in large, hot chunks called clinker.

After the clinker has cooled, a small amount of gypsum (calcium sulfate) is added to it. Then it is crushed into a fine powder. The end result—Portland cement—is stored in silos for future delivery and sale.

Without Portland cement, very little new construction would occur. In 2005, the United States used approximately 134 million tons (121.3 metric tons) of Portland cement.

This unfinished marble statue was carved by the famous Italian artist Michelangelo. Marble was one of his favorite mediums.

It is valued because it can be shaped into strong shapes and blocks, and it can be polished to be smooth and beautiful. Marble can be used in block form. It is also commonly cut into thin layers called veneer. These layers can be laid over cheaper materials to reduce the cost of building. They are also a popular material for kitchen and bathroom countertops.

Iron and Steel

Limestone is an important ingredient in the production of iron and steel. Large quantities of iron ore, coke (a carbon source), and limestone are heated to high temperatures in a blast furnace. This process is called smelting. The limestone in this process is used as a flux. This is a substance that lowers the melting point of another substance. In this case, it lowers the melting point of impurities in the iron ore, particularly silicates.

The limestone joins with these impurities to form a substance called slag. Slag rises to the top of the mixture. The molten iron (and tiny amounts of carbon) sink to the bottom of the mixture. This molten mixture is removed from the furnace. When it cools, it is known as pig iron. Pig iron can be mixed with slag to create wrought iron. Wrought iron is easy to work with when hot. It has been used for centuries by blacksmiths to create horseshoes and tools.

Steel is produced in a blast furnace, like the one shown here. The furnace causes limestone (calcium carbonate) to break down into calcium oxide, which mixes with impurities to form slag.

Pig iron is used to make steel as well. The oldest method of making steel involves an open-hearth furnace. Once again, limestone is mixed with the pig iron to work as a flux. As the mixture is heated, the limestone mixes with the impurities to make slag. The slag is removed from the mixture, leaving one of the strongest materials known to man—steel.

Calcium and Medical Uses

In addition to being employed in popular building materials, calcium compounds have served numerous medical purposes over the centuries. Plaster of Paris has been used for about 1,000 years for casts to hold broken bones in place while they mend. In more recent times, similar plasters were used to make dental casts, although they are not used for this purpose anymore because of the discovery of substances with more desirable qualities. Some antacids (medicines that reduce harmful stomach acid) contain calcium compounds. Also, many toothpastes contain powdered calcium carbonate. This calcium compound helps to scrub plaque off of teeth.

Chapter Five
Calcium and You

Calcium ion is one of the most important nutrients in the human diet. It is also the most abundant mineral in the human body. Nearly all of the calcium ions in our bodies are found in our bones and teeth. About 2 percent is in our muscles, nerves, and other tissues.

Healthy adults require between 1,000 and 1,300 milligrams of calcium (which is the ion, but is commonly just called calcium) in their daily diet. Growing teens should get about 1,300 mg a day. It is crucial for pregnant women and women who are breast-feeding to get plenty of the nutrient to ensure that their babies get the calcium ions they need for proper development. Calcium ions are found in many foods, but they are particularly prevalent in dairy products. A lack of calcium can result in weak teeth and bones, and can even cause the illness rickets. Too much calcium in one's diet over an extended period of time may lead to the formation of kidney stones in those susceptible to them.

Calcium and the Human Body

There are numerous nutrients that the body must have on a daily basis to remain healthy. Calcium ion is one of them. About 98 percent of the calcium ions in the human body are in the bones and teeth. The remaining 2 percent helps to regulate what happens to the other 98 percent. Calcium

Food Sources of Calcium

The chart below lists some good sources of calcium ion and the amount each food contains. Dairy products are among the best sources of calcium ion. However, significant amounts of calcium can be found in some fish (with edible bones), seeds, beans, fruits, and vegetables. (Totals are approximations.)

Food	Portion	Calcium (in mg)
yogurt (low-fat, plain)	1 cup	400
collard greens (cooked)	1 cup	350
milk (whole, 2 percent, 1 percent, skim)	1 cup	300
calcium-fortified orange juice	1 cup	300
canned sardines (with bones)	2 ounces	250
kale (cooked)	1 cup	200
cheddar cheese	1 ounce	200
white beans	1 cup	180
American cheese	1 ounce	160
cottage cheese (1 percent fat)	1 cup	140
tofu (uncooked)	½ cup	130
canned salmon (with bones)	2 ounces	110
sesame seeds	1 tablespoon	90

ions help our nerves and muscles work properly, help our blood clot, and keep our hearts beating regularly. Without calcium ions, we would not be able to live.

Bones

The calcium ions in our bones serve several functions. Most obviously, they make our bones hard and strong. Without calcium ions, our bones would be weak and bendable. Our bones function as calcium ion storehouses. Bones may seem like unchangeable, permanent things, but they are actually being rebuilt constantly. When calcium and phosphate ions are needed somewhere in our bodies, they are taken from our bones. These ions are returned to our bones when we get them in our diets and when there is too much in our bloodstream.

There are several kinds of calcium phosphate compounds in bones. They are all commonly called apatite. Our bones are covered with a very hard layer of calcium carbonate. Bones have a web-like structure made of protein inside them. This framework is filled in with calcium phosphate. This interior area is commonly called bone marrow. It is the softer area through which blood vessels flow. Many bones, like those of the legs, spine, and arms, are hollow, despite being very hard. This hollow center makes them lighter and stronger than if they were solid throughout.

Teeth

Teeth contain the hardest substance in the human body: enamel. It is the outer surface of our teeth. It is made of apatite. Just like our bones, enamel constantly looses calcium and phosphate ions. These ions are replaced by the foods we eat. Our mouths create saliva, which contains calcium and phosphate ions.

The enamel on our teeth can be weakened by a substance called plaque. Plaque is created by bacteria in the mouth. Some kinds of bacteria change plaque into an acid that can eat away at the enamel on teeth. This creates weak spots where bacteria can get inside the teeth. This can lead to cavities and other dental illnesses. By brushing and flossing our teeth regularly, and by controlling the sugar in our diet, we can keep the plaque from building up. This allows saliva to keep up with the bacteria in our mouths, replacing the calcium and phosphate ions necessary to keep our teeth strong and healthy.

Soak an egg in vinegar for twenty-four hours *(1 and 2)*. The vinegar acid releases carbon dioxide (CO_2) gas from the shell, making it soft *(3)*. Later, the shell reforms by taking carbon from the air. This allows the egg to regain its hardness *(4)*.

Blood and Muscle

There is always a small amount of calcium ions in the bloodstream. A little over half of the calcium in the blood is in the form of free calcium ions. The calcium ions in the blood can be moved in and out of the areas of the body where they are needed. The rest are attached to or associated with proteins or other nutrients.

Calcium ions are vital to the clotting of blood. When you are cut, they help the blood to form an important substance to stop the bleeding. This substance forms threads that cover the wound. These threads trap red blood cells and form a clot over the cut. This stops the bleeding. Without calcium ions, this process would not occur, and our cuts would not stop bleeding.

Calcium ions are important to our muscle cells. These cells receive messages from the nervous system. This causes the cells to release calcium ions. Calcium ions tell fiber in the muscles to contract, or tighten. Calcium ions also tell the muscles of the heart to contract, making it possible for the heart to pump blood throughout our bodies.

A Lack of Calcium

Your body does not absorb all of the calcium ions you ingest. Children usually absorb 50 to 70 percent of the calcium ions they take in. This total decreases as a person ages. For this reason, you must include plenty of calcium-rich foods in your diet every day. It is also important to consume a sufficient level of vitamin D, which increases the absorption of calcium ions.

In childhood, a lack of calcium ions in the diet can result in a condition called rickets. Rickets is characterized by legs that bow outward. This is the result of bones that lack enough calcium ions to stay strong and rigid. Rickets is not as common as it once was. Many of the foods we eat—such as milk and orange juice—are fortified with calcium ions and vitamin D. This makes it easier to get our daily allowance of these important nutrients.

A lack of calcium ions can affect adults. Our bones need it to rebuild and stay strong. Older people who lack sufficient calcium ions in their diets may develop osteoporosis. This means that their bones are not as dense as those of healthy people and are more likely to crack. Those with

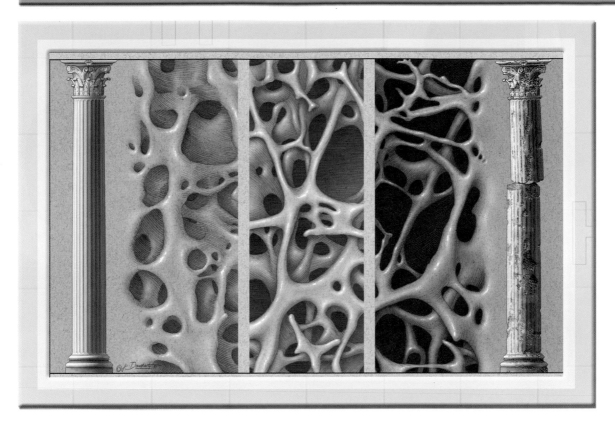

Osteoporosis is the weakening of bone. The Roman columns in this illustration reflect how weak bones can break as bone density is lost.

osteoporosis often have a stooped posture. This is because spinal bones are no longer able to hold up the weight of the body. Older people often take calcium supplements to ensure that they are getting enough of the mineral on a daily basis.

The Periodic Table of Elements

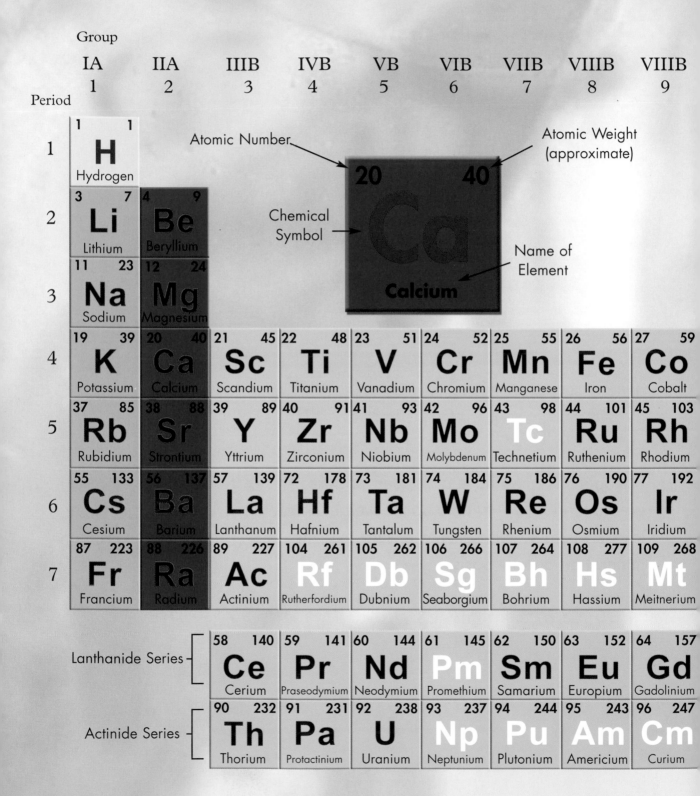

Group

| IA 1 | IIA 2 | IIIB 3 | IVB 4 | VB 5 | VIB 6 | VIIB 7 | VIIIB 8 | VIIIB 9 |

Period

Atomic Number

Atomic Weight (approximate)

20 40

Ca

Chemical Symbol

Name of Element

Calcium

1 — **1 1 H** Hydrogen

2 —
- **3 7 Li** Lithium
- **4 9 Be** Beryllium

3 —
- **11 23 Na** Sodium
- **12 24 Mg** Magnesium

4 —
- **19 39 K** Potassium
- **20 40 Ca** Calcium
- **21 45 Sc** Scandium
- **22 48 Ti** Titanium
- **23 51 V** Vanadium
- **24 52 Cr** Chromium
- **25 55 Mn** Manganese
- **26 56 Fe** Iron
- **27 59 Co** Cobalt

5 —
- **37 85 Rb** Rubidium
- **38 88 Sr** Strontium
- **39 89 Y** Yttrium
- **40 91 Zr** Zirconium
- **41 93 Nb** Niobium
- **42 96 Mo** Molybdenum
- **43 98 Tc** Technetium
- **44 101 Ru** Ruthenium
- **45 103 Rh** Rhodium

6 —
- **55 133 Cs** Cesium
- **56 137 Ba** Barium
- **57 139 La** Lanthanum
- **72 178 Hf** Hafnium
- **73 181 Ta** Tantalum
- **74 184 W** Tungsten
- **75 186 Re** Rhenium
- **76 190 Os** Osmium
- **77 192 Ir** Iridium

7 —
- **87 223 Fr** Francium
- **88 226 Ra** Radium
- **89 227 Ac** Actinium
- **104 261 Rf** Rutherfordium
- **105 262 Db** Dubnium
- **106 266 Sg** Seaborgium
- **107 264 Bh** Bohrium
- **108 277 Hs** Hassium
- **109 268 Mt** Meitnerium

Lanthanide Series
- **58 140 Ce** Cerium
- **59 141 Pr** Praseodymium
- **60 144 Nd** Neodymium
- **61 145 Pm** Promethium
- **62 150 Sm** Samarium
- **63 152 Eu** Europium
- **64 157 Gd** Gadolinium

Actinide Series
- **90 232 Th** Thorium
- **91 231 Pa** Protactinium
- **92 238 U** Uranium
- **93 237 Np** Neptunium
- **94 244 Pu** Plutonium
- **95 243 Am** Americium
- **96 247 Cm** Curium

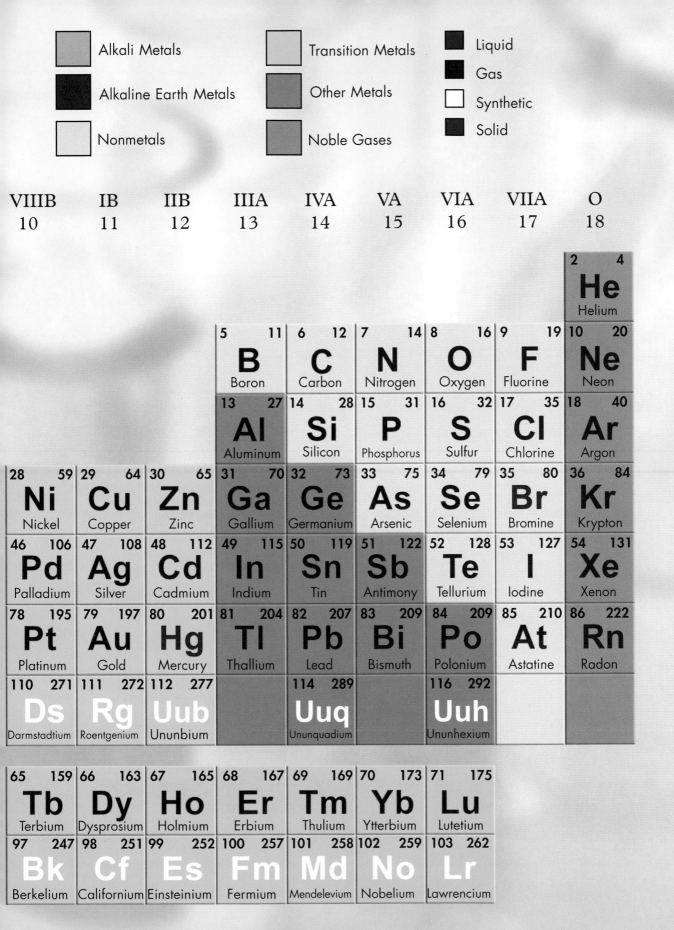

Alkali Metals

Alkaline Earth Metals

Nonmetals

Transition Metals

Other Metals

Noble Gases

Liquid

Gas

Synthetic

Solid

VIIIB 10	IB 11	IIB 12	IIIA 13	IVA 14	VA 15	VIA 16	VIIA 17	O 18

								2 4 **He** Helium
			5 11 **B** Boron	6 12 **C** Carbon	7 14 **N** Nitrogen	8 16 **O** Oxygen	9 19 **F** Fluorine	10 20 **Ne** Neon
			13 27 **Al** Aluminum	14 28 **Si** Silicon	15 31 **P** Phosphorus	16 32 **S** Sulfur	17 35 **Cl** Chlorine	18 40 **Ar** Argon
28 59 **Ni** Nickel	29 64 **Cu** Copper	30 65 **Zn** Zinc	31 70 **Ga** Gallium	32 73 **Ge** Germanium	33 75 **As** Arsenic	34 79 **Se** Selenium	35 80 **Br** Bromine	36 84 **Kr** Krypton
46 106 **Pd** Palladium	47 108 **Ag** Silver	48 112 **Cd** Cadmium	49 115 **In** Indium	50 119 **Sn** Tin	51 122 **Sb** Antimony	52 128 **Te** Tellurium	53 127 **I** Iodine	54 131 **Xe** Xenon
78 195 **Pt** Platinum	79 197 **Au** Gold	80 201 **Hg** Mercury	81 204 **Tl** Thallium	82 207 **Pb** Lead	83 209 **Bi** Bismuth	84 209 **Po** Polonium	85 210 **At** Astatine	86 222 **Rn** Radon
110 271 **Ds** Darmstadtium	111 272 **Rg** Roentgenium	112 277 **Uub** Ununbium	114 289 **Uuq** Ununquadium		116 292 **Uuh** Ununhexium			

65 159 **Tb** Terbium	66 163 **Dy** Dysprosium	67 165 **Ho** Holmium	68 167 **Er** Erbium	69 169 **Tm** Thulium	70 173 **Yb** Ytterbium	71 175 **Lu** Lutetium
97 247 **Bk** Berkelium	98 251 **Cf** Californium	99 252 **Es** Einsteinium	100 257 **Fm** Fermium	101 258 **Md** Mendelevium	102 259 **No** Nobelium	103 262 **Lr** Lawrencium

Glossary

alloy A mixture of two or more elements, at least one of which is a metal.

bacteria One-celled parasitic organisms.

blast furnace An industrial oven heated by very hot jets of air forced into the bottom of the chamber.

caustic Capable of burning the skin or eating away other delicate items by a chemical reaction.

coke A solid material, made mostly of carbon, that remains after coal is burned.

crystal A solid material containing atoms, molecules, or ions that line up in regular, repeated, geometric, three-dimensional patterns.

fortify To add ingredients to a food to make it more nutritional.

geyser A spring that throws a jet of hot water or steam into the air.

glandular Relating to organs in the body that add or remove chemicals from the blood.

hot spring An underground body of water heated by geological activity.

isolate To separate one substance from a mixture of substances.

kidney stone A small, hard mass that sometimes forms in the kidney.

precipitate To cause a solid to form, or to refer to the solid that has formed.

radioactive Describing an element that decays over time by a process involving the nucleus, releasing potentially harmful particles in the process.

silicate Common minerals that contain silicon, oxygen, and one or more other ions.

supplement A substance or medicine taken to make up for a lack of a mineral in one's diet.

# For More Information

American Chemical Society
1155 16th Street NW
Washington, DC 20036
(800) 227-5558
(202) 872-4600
E-mail: webmaster@acs.org
Web site: http://acswebcontent.acs.org/

American Chemistry Council
1300 Wilson Boulevard
Arlington, VA 22209
(703) 741-5000
Web site: http://www.americanchemistry.com/

Chemical Heritage Foundation
315 Chestnut Street
Philadelphia, PA 19106
(215) 925-2222
E-mail: info@chemheritage.org
Web site: http://www.chemheritage.org/

The Electrochemical Society
65 South Main Street, Building D
Pennington, NJ 08534-2839
(609) 737-1902
E-mail: ecs@electrochem.org
Web site: http://www.electrochem.org/

National Osteoporosis Foundation (NOF)
1232 22nd Street NW
Washington, DC 20037-1292
(202) 223-2226
Web site: http://www.nof.org/

Smithsonian Institute
P.O. Box 37012
SI Building, Room 153, MRC 010
Washington, DC 20013-7012
(202) 633-1000
E-mail: info@si.edu
Web site: http://www.si.edu/

Web Sites

Due to the changing nature of Internet links, Rosen Publishing has developed an online list of Web sites related to the subject of this book. This site is updated regularly. Please use this link to access the list:

http://www.rosenlinks.com/uept/calc

For Further Reading

Blashfield, Jean F. *Calcium*. Austin, TX: Raintree Steck-Vaughn, 1999.

Llewellyn, Claire. *Concrete*. New York, NY: Franklin Watts, 2006.

Pough, Frederick H. *Peterson First Guide to Rocks and Minerals*. New York, NY: Houghton Mifflin, 1991.

Stwertka, Albert. *A Guide to the Elements*. Oxford, England: Oxford University Press, 2002.

Tocci, Salvatore. *Calcium*. New York, NY: Children's Press, 2004.

Bibliography

Beaver, Donald. "Iron and Steel." *World Book Multimedia Encyclopedia.* CD-ROM. 2001.

Blashfield, Jean F. *Calcium.* Austin, TX: Raintree Steck-Vaughn, 1999.

Brain, Marshall. "How Iron and Steel Work." HowStuffWorks.com. Retrieved November 30, 2006 (http://science.howstuffworks.com/iron.htm).

BuildEazy.com. "All About Cement." Retrieved November 28, 2006 (http://www.buildeazy.com/newplans/eazylist/cement.html).

DK Staff. *The DK Science Encyclopedia.* New York, NY: DK Publishing, 1998.

Emsley, John. *Nature's Building Blocks: An A–Z Guide to the Elements.* Oxford, England: Oxford University Press, 2001.

Gagnon, Steve. "It's Elemental: Calcium." Thomas Jefferson National Accelerator Facility. Retrieved December 1, 2006 (http://education.jlab.org/itselemental/ele020.html).

Hass, Elson M. "Calcium." HealthWorld.com. Retrieved December 1, 2006 (http://www.healthy.net/scr/article.asp?ID=2019).

Knapp, Brian. *Calcium and Magnesium.* Danbury, CT: Grolier Educational, 1997.

Neal, John A. "Cement and Concrete." *World Book Multimedia Encyclopedia.* CD-ROM. 2001.

Newton, David E. *The Chemical Elements.* New York, NY: Franklin Watts, 1994.

Pough, Frederick H. *Peterson First Guide to Rocks and Minerals.* New York, NY: Houghton Mifflin, 1991.

Schewe, Phil, and Ben Stein. "Elements 116 and 118 Are Discovered." *Physical News Update.* American Institute of Physics. October 16,

2006. Retrieved October 25, 2006 (http://www.aip.org/pnu/2006/797.html).

Stwertka, Albert. *A Guide to the Elements.* Oxford, England: Oxford University Press, 2002.

Wikipedia.com. "Limelight." November 28, 2006. Retrieved December 1, 2006 (http://en.wikipedia.org/wiki/Limelight).

Index

About the Author

Greg Roza has written and edited educational materials for children for the past seven years. He has a master's degree in English from the State University of New York at Fredonia. Roza has long had an interest in scientific topics, including chemistry, and spends much of his spare time tinkering with machines around the house. He lives in Hamburg, New York, with his wife, Abigail, and his three children, Autumn, Lincoln, and Daisy.

Photo Credits

Cover, pp. 1, 13, 14, 16, 38–39 by Tahara Anderson; p. 7 The Art Archive/John Meek; p. 9 © Getty Images; p. 11 © Charles D. Winters/ Photo Researchers, Inc.; p. 19 © Andrew Lambert Photography/Photo Researchers, Inc., p. 21 © Alexis Rosenfeld/Photo Researchers, Inc.; p. 22 Shutterstock.com; p. 23 Mark Golebiowski; p. 25 © James Steinberg/ Photo Researchers, Inc.; p. 28 © Cordelia Molloy/Photo Researchers, Inc.; p. 29 Nimatallah/Art Resource, NY; p. 30 © Paul Shambroom/Photo Researchers, Inc.; p. 35 Cindy Reiman; p. 37 © John M. Daugherty/ Photo Researchers, Inc.

Designer: Tahara Anderson; **Editor:** Nicholas Croce
Photo Researcher: Cindy Reiman